PREPARING FOR BAPTISM IN THE EPISCOPAL CHURCH

ANNE E. KITCH

Morehouse Publishing
NEW YORK

Morehouse Publishing, 4785 Linglestown Road, Suite 101, Harrisburg, PA 17112

Morehouse Publishing, 19 East 34th Street, New York, NY 10016

Morehouse Publishing is an imprint of Church Publishing Incorporated.

www.churchpublishing.org

Cover image: www.hinzfineart.com © 2014 Tim Hinz

Cover design: Laurie Klein Westhafer

Interior design and production: Helen H. Harrison

Library of Congress Cataloging-in-Publication Data
A catalog record of this book is available from the Library of Congress

ISBN 13: 978-0-8192-3171-0 (pbk)

ISBN 13: 978-0-8192-3172-7 (ebook)

Printed in the United States of America

CONTENTS

ACKNOWLEDGEMENTS

I am grateful to Tracey Herzer and Jim Turrell, not only for their contributions to this work, but also for their inestimable influence on the lifelong Christian formation of so many. I also thank Jim for reading early versions of this work and offering his theological expertise. I thank the editorial staff at Church Publishing for all they do, and I am indebted to Sharon Pearson for her vision, encouragement, and editorial wisdom.

A BEGINNING

Water. Ancient words. The Holy Spirit. Baptism. Simply put, Christian baptism is new life. It is a beginning. It is a belonging. It is an initiation. The elements employed in Christian baptism are simple. Water and words. Water that has been blessed by prayer, and ancient words, "I baptize you in the name of the Father, and of the Son, and of the Holy Spirit." Then, of course, comes the inexorable power of the Holy Spirit, sweeping in like a rush of wind to bestow new life.

Water as the outward symbol of baptism seems obvious. Water is necessary for life. All life. Any life. Our bodies consist of up to 80 percent water, while 75 percent of the earth is covered by water. In the book of Genesis, water preexists creation:

> In the beginning when God created the heavens and the earth, the earth was a formless void and darkness covered the face of the deep, while a wind from God swept over the face of the waters. —Genesis 1:1–2

Water is powerful. Human beings can harness it to produce energy. Its rains can dissolve mountains and dig canyons over millennia. Its floods can wipe away entire hillsides in a few minutes. It cleanses and purifies.

Words also convey power. The ancient words of baptism come from scripture. In the final chapter of the Gospel according to Matthew, Jesus leaves his disciples with these words:

> Go therefore and make disciples of all nations, baptizing them in the name of the Father and of the Son and of the Holy Spirit, and teaching them to obey everything that I have commanded you. —Matthew 28:19–20a

From the beginning, the church has used these words in its rites of initiation, invoking the Trinity. Water and words. But what exactly is baptism all about?

Through the sacred rite of Holy Baptism, people enter a new life in Christ. This life is characterized by love and promise. A life in Christ brings with it surety in the goodness of all creation, persistent hope, and regard for compassion, justice, humility, and gentleness. It is abundant with forgiveness, the continual opportunity for renewal and reconciliation, and entrance into the mystery of eternal life. This life is lived out here and now, yet also in the future, as we stand at the threshold of the sacred and believe that our lives can be transformed daily into peace and delight that is beyond suffering. Baptism is a cleansing and a renewal. A beginning and an ongoing story. A liminal moment and an eternal mystery.

This book is about preparing for Christian baptism in The Episcopal Church. While we may hear people say, "I was baptized a Methodist," or "I was baptized Catholic," or "I was baptized an Episcopalian," people are not baptized into a denomination; people are baptized into the Christian faith. While various Christian denominations differ in both their theology of baptism and their rites, faith in Christ is a unifying gift. This book explores baptism as it is understood and practiced in The Episcopal Church following the rite found in the Book of Common Prayer 1979.

WHAT IS BAPTISM?

Holy Baptism is full initiation by water and Holy Spirit into Christ's Body the Church. The bond which God establishes in Baptism is indissoluble. (BCP, p. 298)

Thus baptism is defined in the Book of Common Prayer, the liturgical book of The Episcopal Church. But what does this mean? If we were to dissect this statement, we might point to the word "initiation" as being of obvious importance. We might also be drawn to the word "full." The Episcopal Church claims that baptism is full initiation. Nothing else is needed for membership. Any baptized person, regardless of age, ability, gender, ethnicity, or any other human characteristic, is fully a part of the church. Thus baptism should not be entered into lightly or without preparation.

God is the agent in baptism; God originates this initiation. It is God who establishes the bond. God is the actor here. Through baptism, people are bound to God and God will not let go. Ever. In fact, that bond, made by water and the Holy Spirit, is "indissoluble." It cannot be dissolved. We say that God is faithful. Even as believers, we act unfaithfully toward God all the time. But God never loses faith in us.

Baptism is the result of God's grace, the unearned favor of God. People enter into baptism, or choose to have their children baptized, because they have yearned for God and have begun turning to God in Christ. This turning is the beginning of what Christians call *conversion*, a process in which both God and the seeker take an active part. But make no mistake; it is God the Holy Spirit who confers new life.

Baptism is also a sacrament. In fact, according to the catechism found in the Book of Common Prayer (BCP, pp. 845–862), it is one of two that Jesus initiates. The other is the Eucharist. A sacrament is an outward and visible sign of inward and spiritual grace. The outward and visible sign of baptism is the water along with the words of the triune formula. The inward and spiritual grace conferred by baptism is nothing less than union with Jesus Christ. And this union encompasses birth into God's family, forgiveness of sins, and new life in the Holy Spirit.

And for centuries, people have been willing to take the plunge.

TAKING THE PLUNGE: WHY GET BAPTIZED?

Baptism is never about getting one's feet wet or testing the waters. As Bishop Michael Curry has said, whether the priest sprinkles water on a baptismal candidate or dunks her in a river, baptism is nothing less than full immersion into the power of the Holy Spirit. Why would anyone want to do that?[1]

To choose to be baptized is to choose to enter deeply into a life in Christ. And this means to enter into the mystery of Christ's death and resurrection. Even though the baptism service itself might take place in a beautiful church on a glorious spring morning, the church teaches that through baptism one must actually die to one life in order to be born into another. Those baptized die to a life that is not centered on Christ, so as to be born anew into one that makes no sense without the love of Christ.

The Christian life is about more than a set of values. It is about believing that Christ conquered sin and death. It is about the assurance that comes with having a savior who has suffered the worst the world has to offer, has overcome death, and has risen to respond in love. The Christian life is about more than getting into heaven. It is about choosing to love others each day because God first loved us, and because all people are God's beloved. The Christian life is about feeding the hungry, finding the lost, comforting the bereft, healing the broken, setting free the oppressed. The Christian life is about making a difference in the world each day. It is about loving God and loving one's neighbor—and one's neighbor turns out to be everybody. The Christian life demands all of one's being.

And the Christian life makes sense out of all of one's being. Choosing to be baptized is to choose to be transformed by love over and over again for a lifetime. And beyond.

---

[1] From an address by the Rt. Rev. Michael Curry given at St. Stephen's Pro-Cathedral, Wilkes-Barre, PA, on May 14, 2011.

THE CREEDS AND ANCIENT PRACTICES

Choosing to be baptized is also to take on a particular set of beliefs. Creeds are statements of belief; in fact, the word "creed" comes from the Latin *credo* or "I believe." The Episcopal Church uses two creeds in worship: the Apostles' Creed and the Nicene Creed. The Nicene Creed was developed at the Council of Nicea in 325 and is a sophisticated theological statement about basic Christian tenants. The Apostles' Creed is more ancient, its very name deriving from a story that the first apostles themselves each wrote a line. What is known about the Apostles' Creed is that it is not only a statement of belief, but also an ancient baptismal formula. In the early church, a Christian baptism might have looked something like the following:

Having spent several months or even years of instruction in the Christian faith and practices, an adult would be ready for baptism. On the day of the baptism, the converts would first be taken to a baptistry adjoining the main worship area. There, they would be asked about their belief, "Do you believe in God the Father?" They would respond with the formulaic lines that they had been taught, but which also encapsulated the theological understanding of the first person of the Trinity. Having answered, they would then be submerged into the water.

They would then be asked, "Do you believe in Jesus Christ, the Son of God?" Their affirmative response would be followed by a second submersion. Finally, they would be asked, "Do you believe in God the Holy Spirit?" and upon answering with the last part of the creed they would undergo a third submersion. Then the newly baptized would each be clothed in a clean white garment as a sign of new birth, and led in procession to the church where the community would already be gathered in prayer. There they would be welcomed and immediately join in the celebration of the Eucharist, receiving communion for the first time.

Even have spent up to three years in instruction in the Christian faith, the newly baptized did not consider themselves mature Christians. Rather they, and the community of believers, knew that they would continue to grow into the full stature of Christ. They were practicing Christians—followers of Christ who practiced every day.

Then, as today, what follows baptism is lifelong formation in the Christian faith as a disciple of Jesus.

THE APOSTLES' CREED

I believe in God, the Father almighty,
    creator of heaven and earth.

I believe in Jesus Christ, his only Son, our Lord.
    He was conceived by the power of the Holy Spirit
        and born of the Virgin Mary.
    He suffered under Pontius Pilate,
        was crucified, died, and was buried.
    He descended to the dead.
    On the third day he rose again.
    He ascended into heaven,
        and is seated at the right hand of the Father.
    He will come again to judge the living and the dead.

I believe in the Holy Spirit,
    the holy catholic Church,
    the communion of saints,
    the forgiveness of sins,
    the resurrection of the body,
    and the life everlasting. Amen.

A BRIEF HISTORY OF BAPTISM

by James F. Turrell

Through the Paschal mystery, dear friends, we are buried with Christ by Baptism into his death, and raised with him to newness of life. (BCP, p. 292)

While most Christian groups baptize (a notable exception being the Quakers), there has been considerable diversity in the rite's practice and theology. Some of the diversity has centered around performance: Whom should be baptized? Who may perform the baptism? What additional ceremonies might be added to the water bath? How much water to use? Other debated questions have involved the rite's meaning: How are we to understand this sacrament? Is baptism the only initiatory sacrament, or does something (for example, confirmation) need to follow? Perhaps the most foundational question has been whether baptism is efficacious: Does it actually *do* anything? Various Christian communities, in various times, have answered these questions in sharply divergent ways.

Some of this variety is perhaps inevitable, given that the earliest picture of baptism is murky. There is no clear evidence in the New Testament that Jesus himself ever baptized others (apart from a stray reference in John 3:22, which seems to be contradicted a few verses later at 4:2). Jesus's command to baptize, in Matthew 28:19, may or may not be an editorial insertion. Paul's letters presume a pre-existing practice of baptism, but he himself does not describe the ritual practices used. The Acts of the Apostles, at least, describes several baptisms, but the picture

is varied. For example, the neophytes (beginners) that Philip the deacon baptized did not receive the Holy Spirit, in a situation that was regarded as so unusual that the apostles needed later to impose hands in a sort of remedial action (8:14–17). But in the case of the Ethiopian eunuch (8:26–40), there was no subsequent handlaying by the apostles, so presumably Philip was apparently able to confer the Spirit that time. To complicate matters further, sometimes the Spirit came before baptism, as in Acts 10. There is, in short, no clear biblical picture of baptism.

While we have better evidence about ritual process in the second and subsequent centuries, we find considerable diversity until at least the fourth century. Some sources, such as the Didache, described a liturgy in which the only ritual action was the water bath.[1] Others, such as the Didascalia, described a sequence of ritual actions, beginning with the anointing of the head and body and concluding with the water bath.[2] The pre-bath anointing was the more important part of the rite, thought to convey the Holy Spirit.[3] In North Africa, by contrast, the sequence was reversed. The water bath came first, followed by anointing.[4] Infant baptism was practiced, but adult baptism was more common, if only because many more came into the church through conversion than through being born to

---

[1] Maxwell E. Johnson, *The Rites of Christian Initiation: Their Evolution and Interpretation*, rev. ed. (Collegeville, MN: Liturgical Press, 2007), 44–5.

[2] Johnson, *Rites of Christian Initiation*, 53–4.

[3] Gabriele Winkler, "The Original Meaning of the Prebaptismal Anointing and Its Implications," in Maxwell Johnson, ed., *Living Water, Sealing Spirit: Readings on Christian Initiation* (Collegeville, MN: Liturgical Press, 1995), 58–75; Aidan Kavanagh, *The Shape of Baptism: The Rite of Christian Initiation*, Studies in the Reformed Rites of the Catholic Church (Collegeville, MN: Liturgical Press, 1978), 42, 47.

[4] Johnson, *Rites of Christian Initiation*, 84–95.

Christian parents. Adult candidates participated in a period of preparation called the catechumenate, which varied in length from three weeks to forty days.[5]

In the fourth and fifth centuries, the baptismal rites across the church came into greater congruence. Most of the Eastern baptismal rites shifted to add a post-bath anointing, along the lines of the Western rites. These post-bath anointings were seen as giving the Holy Spirit, and their pre-bath anointings were re-interpreted as exorcistic[6] (driving out evil forces). In the West, elaborate pre-bath ceremonies, including exorcistic anointings, were added.[7] In Rome, one post-bath was performed by a presbyter, while a second anointing seems to have been reserved to the bishop. In the rest of the West, a presbyter could do all of the anointing. Baptism took place in the context of the Eucharist, so that the neophytes received communion for the first time directly after the bath and anointing, in a unified initiatory rite. Infants as well as adults experienced this unified rite; all who were baptized were also anointed and communicated.[8]

In subsequent centuries, this unified rite broke apart in the West. First, pressure mounted to get baptism done sooner rather than later, largely as a result of increased anxiety about original sin.[9] Also, the Roman rite became the dominant liturgical pattern in the West, so that the norm of a bishop's post-bath anointing spread, usually experienced as an addition, rather than a breaking-off of an episcopal action from a unified rite.[10] Finally, the relative lack of bishops in much of Western Europe (outside the Italian peninsula, medieval dioceses were not particularly compact, in geographical terms) meant that presbyters still performed many baptisms, even as a post-bath anointing was reserved to bishops. The result was a two-stage structure of initiation, with baptism by a presbyter and a subsequent handlaying and anointing by the bishop. The latter rite came to be called "confirmation."

It is important to note that confirmation, in the Middle Ages, had nothing to do with age or education. One was supposed to be confirmed as soon as possible after baptism. Medieval art portrayed infants as the appropriate subjects of confirmation.[11] Further, because of distance and inconvenience (for both bishop and laity), confirmation was rarely performed. Thirteenth-century legislation in England asserted that no one should receive communion until they had been confirmed, in an attempt to make confirmation more widely observed.[12] (From the available evidence, it seems that it had no effect whatsoever.)

---

[5] Johnson, *Rites of Christian Initiation*, 201–18; Maxwell E. Johnson, "From Three Weeks to Forty Days: Baptismal Preparation and the Origins of Lent," in Johnson, ed., *Living Water, Sealing Spirit*, 129–32; Paul Turner, *Ages of Initiation: The First Two Christian Millenia* (Collegeville, MN: Liturgical Press, 2000), 6, 9.

[6] Maxwell E. Johnson, "Baptism and Chrismation in Third- and Fourth-Century Egypt: The State of the Question," *Worship* 88 (2014), 326–7; Winkler, "Original Meaning of the Prebaptismal Anointing," 75–80; Paul F. Bradshaw, "Baptismal Practice in the Alexandrian Tradition: Eastern or Western?" in Johnson, ed., *Living Water, Sealing Spirit*, 93–4.

[7] Johnson, *Rites of Christian Initiation*, 160–67.

[8] Johnson, *Rites of Christian Initiation*, 159–200.

[9] J.D.C. Fisher, *Christian Initiation: Baptism in the Medieval West* (London: Alcuin Club, 1965; Chicago: Liturgy Training Publications, 2004), 123–26.

[10] Johnson, *Rites of Christian Initiation*, 251.

[11] Ann Eljenholm Nichols, *Seeable Signs: The Iconography of the Seven Sacraments, 1350–1544* (Woodbridge, Suffolk, 1994), 207–10.

Confirmation was rarely practiced and widely ignored in the Middle Ages.

At the same time that the post-bath anointing in the unified initiatory rite had split off, first communion came to be delayed as well. Over the course of the Middle Ages, communion came, in the popular imagination, to be tied to private confession of sins to the priest ("auricular confession"), something in which infants did not take part. Various ages were used for first confession, with the age of seven being mandated only as late as the first decades of the twentieth century; but, in any case, first communion was clearly separated from baptism, beginning in the Middle Ages.[13]

The separation of baptism, confirmation, and first communion persisted in the early modern period, though various groups found different solutions for confirmation. Roman Catholics moved the age of confirmation later, so that children or youth, rather than infants, were confirmed. They also allowed, from at least the eighteenth century, presbyters with a "faculty" (a license) to perform confirmations, rather than reserving the rite to bishops.[14] Lutherans retained confirmation but reinterpreted it as a ritualized examination in the catechism by the local pastor, after instruction. Continental Calvinists rejected it entirely. In England, Thomas Cranmer substantially revised confirmation in the 1549 and 1552 Books of Common Prayer. He reserved confirmation to bishops and retained the thirteenth century assertion that it was required before communion, but he

reinterpreted it along Lutheran lines: confirmation followed instruction, and the appropriate candidates were youth. For all of these groups, first communion was delayed after baptism. In practice, confirmation was largely ignored until the 1680s, while catechizing was insisted upon as the essential prerequisite for communion. In any case, though, a two-tiered standard for church membership applied—baptism was insufficient for full, participatory membership in the church. This pattern persisted in Anglicanism until The Episcopal Church produced its 1979 prayer book.

The Protestant reformers substantially revised their baptismal theology and procedure. Martin Luther, in successive revisions, pared down some of the ceremonies inherited from the medieval rite. John Calvin and Ulrich Zwingli produced much more austere rites, and they argued that the only efficacy of baptism lay in bringing a child into the covenant—it did not convey any grace. The Anabaptists went still further, rejecting infant baptism and insisting that only adult believers could be baptized.[15]

In the English Reformation, Thomas Cranmer's first prayer book made only light revisions to the medieval baptismal rite, but his prayer book of 1552 made significant changes. The 1549 rite retained a pre-bath exorcism and a post-bath, presbyteral anointing, while the 1552 book eliminated both. The rite was dramatically simplified: even the blessing of the water was cut. All "superstitious" elements, in Cranmer's eyes, were eliminated (though there would

---

[12] Fisher, 138, 146–47.

[13] Fisher, 114–118; Johnson, *Rites of Christian Initiation*, 262–64.

[14] Gerald Austin, *The Rite of Confirmation: Anointing with the Spirit*, Studies in the Reformed Rites of the Catholic Church (New York: Pueblo Publishing Co., 1985), 47.

[15] Johnson, *Rite of Christian Initiation*, 322–28, 331–40.

be subsequent conflict over a signing with the cross that Cranmer retained and placed after the bath). In one sense, Cranmer's rite had a very different theological underpinning than its predecessors: there was no sense in which the material used in the ritual had changed—the water was still ordinary water—and the core of the rite was the ritual proclamation of God's promise and the people's response in faith. There was also, in general, much less "stuff" used, as anointings, candles, and white garments were dropped. But in another sense, the practice of the rite remained quite similar to its predecessor, as the rite assumed infant candidates, and the theology of the rite was oriented around the cleansing from sin. This Cranmerian focus on washing sin off infants remained the norm in Anglican baptism until the twentieth century.

The twentieth century Liturgical Movement, which reshaped liturgical theology and practice across the churches of the West, radically reoriented baptism. Prompted in part by a renewed focus on early liturgical texts, which showed a unified initiatory rite, both the Roman Catholic and Episcopal churches produced liturgies that reassembled the broken bits of Christian initiation, with water bath, post-bath handlaying (and anointing), and first communion. The Roman Catholic "Rite of Christian Initiation of Adults" proved remarkably influential, as well, in fostering a revival of the catechumenate, the lengthy period of preparation for adult candidates that had first developed in the early church.[16] The trial liturgies produced in 1970 as part of prayer book revision in The Episcopal Church restored handlaying to baptism and would have eliminated the separate rite of confirmation entirely,

but many bishops of the church opposed the loss of their monopoly on confirmation. The final version of the 1979 prayer book included both a unified initiatory rite—with water bath, handlaying and (optional) anointing, and first communion in one liturgy—and a separate rite of confirmation, now labeled simply a "pastoral" office. To eliminate ambiguity, the prayer book asserted that baptism was now "full initiation"—an important rejection of the Cranmerian approach to initiation that still held sway in most of the Anglican Communion at the time. Similarly, the "liturgical norm" of the 1979 prayer book (with norm defined as that which gives shape and meaning to the rite) is the baptism of adult candidates, rather than infants—again, a departure from Cranmerian patterns and Anglican practice. Finally, the content of the rite came to be focused more on the obligations of Christian life, rather than merely the removal of original sin. While it maintained language concerning the cleansing from sin, the new rite underscored that baptism was now also about discipleship.

The practice of baptism, then, has come full circle. Beginning with a unified initiatory rite and adult candidates, the church then fragmented the rite and focused its baptismal attentions on infants. Finally, twentieth-century liturgical reforms restored the ancient pattern, producing the prayer book that we know today. Authentic baptismal practice in The Episcopal Church today must recognize this historical arc, and cannot use the present rites as if they were those in the 1928 prayer book, focused on washing sin from infants. Instead, the liturgy presumes that baptism is about God's grace given

---

[16] RCIA also required that, in the absence of a bishop, the parish priest was to "confirm" the newly baptized, performing the post-bath anointing. [National Conference of Catholic Bishops, *Rite of Christian Initiation of Adults*, study ed. (Collegeville, MN: Liturgical Press, 1985), 7.]

and received, and about our life-changing promises made in response.

About the Author:

James F. Turrell is professor of liturgy at the School of Theology of the University of the South, where he also serves as associate dean. The author of Celebrating the Rites of Initiation (New York: Church Publishing Incorporated, 2013), he is a canon of the Episcopal Diocese of Bethlehem.

BAPTISM OF ADULTS

There is one body and one Spirit, just as you were called to the one hope of your calling, one Lord, one faith, one baptism, one God and Father of all, who is above all and through all and in all. . . . But each of us was given grace according to the measure of Christ's gift. The gifts he gave were that some would be apostles, some prophets, some evangelists, some pastors and teachers, to equip the saints for the work of ministry, for building up the body of Christ, until all of us come to the unity of the faith and of the knowledge of the Son of God, to maturity, to the measure of the full stature of Christ. —Ephesians 4:4–7, 11–13

It is easy to be a member of The Episcopal Church and think that baptism is primarily for infants or very young children. Many adults in the church were themselves baptized as infants, and one can certainly grow up in The Episcopal Church without ever witnessing an adult baptism. However, while baptizing infants and young children may seem the norm in The Episcopal Church, both tradition and the theology of the Book of Common Prayer show a preference for adult baptism.

After all, those first baptized in the name of Jesus were mostly adults. Scripture does contain stories of entire households being baptized, which presumably would have included people of many ages, as the early Christians were spreading a new faith in the world. But the majority of converts were adults who had heard the preaching and teaching of the first apostles and were inspired to commit themselves to the new life offered by Jesus.

Today, many adults come to baptism because they are seeking meaning. Sometimes an important life event, such as the birth of a child or an experience of tragedy, compels a person to ask questions such as "What is my life about?" or "Where is God in all this?" A person can slowly or suddenly discover a hunger for God, and may yearn for a life that, as the apostle Paul describes, can be lived "with all humility and gentleness, with patience, bearing with one another in love, making every effort to maintain the unity of the Spirit in the bond of peace." (Eph. 4:2–3)

In The Episcopal Church, an adult preparing for baptism is called a *catechumen*. This word, coming from the Greek κατηχούμενος, means one being instructed. From ancient times it was understood that adult converts to the Christian faith should undergo a period of instruction and immersion in the principles and practices of the faith before being baptized. As baptism is initiation into the Christian faith, it is sensible that a time of education precede the baptism. One ought to know and understand what kind of promises one is going to make. But baptism is also a response to conversion, and conversion to faith in Christ is God's action. Part of baptismal preparation is becoming more deeply aware of God's work in one's life. Instruction also happens through experience, and in particular the experience one has within a Christian faith community. This process of instruction and experience is formally called the *catechumenate*, although not every Episcopal church uses this term.

THE CATECHUMENATE

When a person enters the catechumenate she is asked:

> "What do you seek?"
> And the answer. . . "Life in Christ."

The catechumen is a seeker, and in this case, someone who is seeking a new and particular kind of life. The catechumen learns about and experiences a life in Christ in the context of a Christian community, most often in a congregation that gathers weekly for worship. Within this community the catechumen not only undergoes formal instruction, but also begins to learn firsthand of the lifesaving power of the gospel. Gospel means "good news," and in the Christian context it refers both to the four scriptural accounts of the life of Jesus found in the Bible (Matthew, Mark, Luke, and John) and to the belief that all life is redeemed through the loving sacrifice of Jesus Christ. Through the stories and life experiences of the other members of the congregation, the catechumen begins to appreciate what this new life in Christ is all about, and how it makes a difference in everyday living. Through exposure to and the study of scripture, the catechumen begins to see the unfolding of God's saving acts through history.

The catechumenate unfolds in three stages:

❖ **The Pre-catechumenal Period**—during which a person is introduced to the Christian faith and recognizes a desire to be baptized.

❖ **The Catechumenate**—in which a person is formally enrolled as a catechumen and begins a period of instruction in scripture and Christian practices and participation in a faith community.

❖ **Candidacy for Baptism**—a series of ceremonies or rites that take place within the parish or worshiping community on the Sundays leading to the baptism itself.

Not every Episcopal church uses the formal catechumenate program. Nevertheless, the components of preparation for baptism should include experience of and reflection on scripture, Christian prayer, and worship. There should be opportunity to gain understanding of the mission of the church and how that mission is particularly lived out in one's congregation, as well as for exploration of the seeker's own gifts for ministry. Also important is instruction in the basic tenants of faith, the creeds, the sacraments, and church governance. Such preparation might well include study of "An Outline of the Faith" found in the Book of Common Prayer (also known as the "Catechism"), which is written in question and answer form as it is intended to be a resource for instruction. In The Episcopal Church we understand that all the baptized are ministers, are able and called to bear witness to the love of Christ, and have gifts to participate in Christ's work of reconciling love. (BCP, p. 855)

Whatever program of preparation is used, this is a process closely connected to one's experience of conversion, and there is no set time frame in which it takes place. However, a year would be a good estimate. Certainly much depends on the person seeking baptism as well as the practices of the parish to which he or she belongs. This time can be seen as a joyous time and a freeing time, when the seeker sets aside a particular to-do list and gives herself over to being loved and formed by God's call to a life in Christ. So many processes in today's world are both regimented and rushed. The church offers a place and space where one is encouraged to delve into a time of curiosity and yearning without reproach. The waters of baptism are inviting and powerful, and one can walk along the shore getting one's feet wet and feeling the tug of the tide for as long as one likes before taking the plunge.

BEING A DISCIPLE

Adult baptism is about becoming a disciple, a follower. Being a follower of Jesus comes with certain responsibilities. Jesus is clear in his teaching that there is an ethic for his followers, which is most clearly expressed in what is known as the two great commandments: Love God with all your heart and soul and strength, and love your neighbor as yourself (Matthew 22:37–40, Mark 12:29–31, Luke 10:25–28).

Preparing for baptism is not just about learning the words of the creed, or becoming familiar with how a congregation worships. It is about being formed in the faith, and beginning to absorb "Christian understandings of God, human relationships, and the meaning of life…"[1]

Christian formation includes learning the Christian story, practicing prayer, worshipping in community, and exploring one's gifts for ministry. Christian formation continues after baptism, as the newly baptized encounters the mystery of faith again and again. Christian formation is, in fact, lifelong.

Baptism is full initiation, but living into one's baptism takes a lifetime. Being a Christian is not just about going to church or holding certain values. It is a way of life. In its best practice, it is a way of life that brings love, hope, and a holy purpose to everyday life.

---

[1] *Book of Occasional Services* (New York: Church Publishing, 2003), 114.

BAPTISM OF CHILDREN

O God, you have taught us through your blessed Son that whoever receives a little child in the name of Christ receives Christ himself: We give you thanks for the blessing your have bestowed upon this family in giving them a child. Confirm their joy by a lively sense of your presence with them, and give them calm strength and patient wisdom as they seek to bring this child to love all that is true and noble, lovable and gracious, excellent and admirable, following the example of our Lord and Savior, Jesus Christ. Amen. (BCP, p. 443)

Choosing to have one's child baptized is a question of faith. Not only is it a decision that commits parents to raising their child in the faith, it is also a faithful decision, a kind of leap of faith. Parenting itself is an exciting journey with many unexpected twists and turns, and the Christian life is also full of surprises. The Book of Common Prayer assumes that faithful parenting comes with the "gift and heritage of children." Children are to be nurtured "in the knowledge and love of the Lord" and the community of faith prays that parents are afforded the grace to bring their children up to know, love, and serve God. (BCP, pp. 429, 423)

Parents are encouraged to bring their child to the congregation to be welcomed, as soon as possible after adoption or birth. This welcoming can be formal, using the service "A Thanksgiving for the Birth or Adoption of a Child" (BCP, 439–445), which is distinct from baptism. This rite can also be used in the hospital or home. Support for the family in their life in Christ has already begun as the congregation prays that God will confirm the parents' joy. Thus, even before a child is baptized, parents and the faith community alike anticipate the gifts that come with a life in Christ.

Parents seek baptism for their child for a variety of reasons. Some do it out of a sense of tradition or family expectation; some do it out of a desire for their child to have a vibrant life of faith; most do it out of love. Most parents choose baptism because they want something good for their child. When asked what they hope the result of their parenting will be, parents respond that they want their children to grow up to be responsible. Caring. Happy. Concerned for others. Compassionate. Able and willing to make good choices. Loving. Parents who seek baptism for their children have a sense that being part of a community of faith will help them raise their children to be all of these things. And they are not wrong.

To enter into Christian baptism is a choice; and in the case of infants or very young children, it is a choice that parents are making for their children. Like choosing what music to play in the nursery, or what foods to introduce their children to, or what activities to enroll them in, baptism is a parenting decision. Ultimately, it is about how to raise a child, and parents who choose baptism are choosing to raise their children with an active faith life.

The faith life of any parent is unique. Thus, how any parent envisions spirituality as part of her or his child's life differs. Yet, when several different parents bring their children to an Episcopal church on a given Sunday for the sacrament of baptism, they will all meet within the same community, at the same font, for the same ritual.

WHY BAPTIZE A BABY?

With an understanding that baptism is a choice, and a commitment to a new life in Christ, and that the initiation includes promises that are made, and that the Book of Common Prayer shows a preference for adult baptism, why do we baptize infants in The Episcopal Church? After all, the catechism, or teaching, of The Episcopal Church states that at baptism individuals are required to renounce Satan, repent of sins, and accept Jesus as Lord and Savior (BCP, p. 858). Infants can do none of these things.

So the obvious question is, why are infants baptized at all? Why not just bless them and allow them to make a choice about their baptism when they are older?

The answer is really twofold.

First, infants are baptized so that they can be full members of the community of faith, the Body of Christ, and can grow up being formed by that fellowship and sharing in all the benefits. Children are honored as complete human beings in The Episcopal Church, and they are considered worthy of "citizenship in the Covenant" (BCP, p. 858), that is the sacred agreement between God and God's people.

But it is perhaps even more important to remember that God acts in baptism. Never underestimate the power of God. We may think that an infant has neither understanding of what is happening in the baptismal rite

nor any capacity to make the required promises. But we have no idea how God is acting in that child's life. Children are born with a physical body, an emotional and psychological make-up, and a spirituality as well. Whether as adults we can perceive it or not, children enter this world with a relationship with God and God is already working in their lives. It is the Christian belief that all human beings are created in the image of God. Even infants have a faith life. To deny this, or to assume that they need to be of a certain age or ability to engage in a life of faith, is to treat them as less than fully human.

What infant baptism is *not* is some kind of divine protection system. God loves all of God's creation and all of God's creatures, including each human being, whether baptized or not. While some parents may fear that an unbaptized child who dies will not go to heaven, this is simply not the teaching of The Episcopal Church (see "A Brief History of Baptism," pp. 10–14). Parents who choose to have their infants or young children baptized often articulate that at some level they see baptism as a form of protection. Even adults might approach baptism with this idea in mind.

Baptism is really not about holy fire insurance. Rather it is about how one lives every day. The focus of the baptismal rite in the Book of Common Prayer 1979 is about making disciples. It is about being a follower of Christ.

WHAT PARENTS AND GODPARENTS PROMISE

Parents and godparents are asked to make significant promises on behalf of a child they are sponsoring for baptism. First and foremost, these adults are asked to make two very significant promises about the life of the child they are to present:

❖ Will you be responsible for seeing that the child you present is brought up in the Christian faith and life?

❖ Will you, by your prayers and witness, help this child to grow into the full stature of Christ?

If nothing else, these two promises make it clear that baptizing a child is about entrance into the Christian life and that the role of parents and godparents is to raise this child in the faith.

The first promise is about responsibility. An infant cannot make choices about what forms her; she is dependent on the adults around her to make those choices. Having chosen to have a child baptized, parents then take on the first responsibility for teaching her about a life in Christ and providing those experiences that will form her faith. This includes bringing her to the gatherings of the faith community for worship, fellowship, and teaching. Parents and godparents live out this promise when they introduce a child to the stories of the faith, share with her the teachings of Jesus, and teach her about Christian faith practices such as prayer, generosity, and service to others.

The second promise commits parents and godparents to practicing their own faith. Like any of the rest of us, children learn by doing and are formed by the environment around them. Practicing prayer in the home, such as grace at meals and bedtime prayers, is one way to witness the love of Christ to a child. Reading Bible stories together, celebrating Christian holidays in the home, following the seasons of the church year, and practicing charity together are all ways that adults can witness to the love of Christ and help a child grow in faith.

Being part of a community of faith is important as well. Very young infants can absorb the sights and smells and sounds around them. Bringing children to worship exposes them to the beauty and practice of ritual. Participating in church activities also introduces a child to her extended Christian family.

The baptism of a child is an opportunity for the parents and godparents to deepen their own faith as well. During the baptismal liturgy, parents and godparents renew their commitment to Christ by renouncing Satan, repenting of their sins, and turning to Jesus as their Savior. All of this is done surrounded by the community of faith, who witness these promises, pray for the parents and those about to be baptized, and commit to supporting them in their life in Christ. This is why baptisms occur during the principle Eucharist on a Sunday (or feast day) and it is inappropriate for a non-emergency baptism to take place privately—so that all those participating know they are surrounded by a loving community that enjoys with them the promises and challenges of the Christian life.

PREPARING CHILDREN FOR BAPTISM

Almighty God, heavenly Father, you have blessed us with the joy and care of children: Give us calm strength and patient wisdom as we bring them up, that we may teach them to love whatever is just and true and good, following the example of our Savior Jesus Christ. Amen. (BCP, p. 829)

Regardless of whether children are infants, toddlers, or older, there are simple ways parents can prepare them for their baptism. The most important thing a parent can do is to explain to a child what is happening and why. Some parents may feel intimidated about this, because they don't think they have a good enough understanding of the sacrament of baptism. But a theological education is not necessary. Parents can begin by simply telling a child, in their own words, why baptism and a life of faith are important to them and why they are choosing baptism for their child. We share our hopes with our children all the time, even whispering words of love into the tiny ears of sleeping infants. It is never too early to share with children the love we have found in Jesus.

Parents can also respect their children by telling them what will happen during the baptismal liturgy itself. Again, whether they are infants or school age, children are more comfortable if they know what a ceremony is all about and what is expected of them; after all, this is true for adults as well!

Many parents wonder at what age a child should be baptized. There is no one right answer to this. Some parents want their children to be baptized as soon after birth as possible; others want their children to be old enough to choose the Christian life for themselves. Some children become part of a Christian family through adoption at an older age, and are baptized when the time seems right. Some children are members of households that become Christian and are baptized along with their parents. It is helpful to remember that children (or parents for that matter) do not need to "understand" what baptism is about in the moment in order to receive its full benefits; infants are baptized all the time and joyfully raised in the faith. Baptisms should be planned thoughtfully and without a sense of urgency; there is no need to rush to the font. In the case of infants, it may be practical to choose a time when sleep deprivation of new parents and crankiness of a newborn do not overwhelm the joy of the occasion. The timing of a baptism might also depend on whether the family belongs to a congregation in which the child's faith can be nurtured and the parents can be supported.

Whenever the baptism is to take place, these are some simple ways to prepare children for the holy event:

❖ Take a tour of the church in which the baptism is to take place, especially exploring the baptismal font.

❖ Look for baptismal symbols that may be in the church or near the font such as sea shells, a dove, signs of the Trinity, icons, or stained-glass windows depicting the Baptism of Christ.

❖ Review with your child all the steps of the service, what will happen, and what to expect.

❖ Explain how water will be used in the baptism. Will it be poured on the forehead or will the child be immersed?

❖ Choose clothing for the baptism that is both comfortable and celebratory for the child.

❖ If children are old enough, let them have a choice in what they will wear that makes them feel special. If a child will wear a family baptismal gown, explain to him where it comes from and who has worn it before.

❖ Tell the story of other family baptisms, like those of the parents, siblings, cousins, or godparents.

❖ Tell all these stories to infants even if you think they cannot understand.

❖ Read books together about baptism (see Resources on p. 48).

A NOTE ABOUT OLDER CHILDREN

The baptismal rite of The Episcopal Church indicates that children who are old enough should speak for themselves, rather than having parents and godparents speak for them. When are children old enough to speak for themselves? This is a judgment call, which is why a particular age is not given. Certainly, young children are able to have a relationship with God and to express their yearning for a closer connection to God. Parents can lovingly discuss this with their child and let her choose if she feels ready to speak for herself. Children who express a desire to be baptized and can speak for themselves are presented for baptism along with adult candidates. Parents still play a pivotal role in formation, and act as baptismal sponsors along with godparents, but do not make promises on behalf of the child.

GODPARENTS

by Tracey E. Herzer

God our Father, you see your children growing up in an unsteady and confusing world: Show them that your ways give more life than the ways of the world, and that following you is better than chasing after selfish goals. Help them to take failure, not as a measure of their worth, but as a chance for a new start. Give them strength to hold their faith in you, and to keep alive their joy in your creation; through Jesus Christ our Lord. Amen. (BCP, p. 829)

Parenting is wondrous, amazing, dangerous, remarkable, scary, magical stuff. And perhaps never more so than when tackling life's biggest questions: Who is God? Who are we? Why do things happen we can't explain? As children grow and change, parents continually encounter these and other hard questions in their children's lives, and in their own. Parents play an important role in helping children observe the world and learn to recognize their role in things. Parents also nurture their children's innate, authentic relationship with their loving Creator. These experiences are vital to helping children understand how faith (and their Baptismal Covenant) plays a part in everyday life, but navigating them as a parent can also sometimes be difficult. . . and that is why godparents are so important.

CHOOSING GODPARENTS

The word "godparent" is used in many different ways. In some families, the term is used to denote the people who would have guardianship over a child should something happen to the parents. Other families use the word as an indicator of a close familial relationship, but not necessarily a spiritual role. However, in the eyes of the church, a godparent is someone who stands as a sponsor with parents at a child's baptism, promising to support by prayer and example as the child begins her new life in Christ.

When considering godparents for a child, it helps to be clear with potential candidates about roles and expectations. Godparents do not need to be theological scholars, nor do they need to be present every day in a child's life to make a big impact. What is probably most helpful is to choose people with the willingness to "swim in deep waters" and a comfort level with talking about big subjects like life, death, God, and love. Godparents don't need to be people who have the answers—because no one does—but rather folks who aren't intimidated by questions and who will love and support children when they begin to wrestle with things.

Sometimes godparents are chosen based solely on friendships or family ties without pausing to think about the sacred responsibility they are asked to undertake. In choosing a godparent, it is important to consider their ability to follow through on the promises they will be making to see that the child is brought up in the Christian faith and life. In big question moments, it is a wonderful blessing to have a godparent who can sit quietly when there aren't easy answers or will stand in the gap with a child as she navigates something that is unknown or unknowable. Often when parents choose godparents, they look at a tiny baby and imagine a beautiful life with only a few minor bumps along the way. But most people find that life unfolds a bit differently and godparents can help parents respond faithfully and prayerfully to whatever life brings. Godparents might be there to give extra hugs or offer a special prayer when a beloved family pet dies. Or they may send a note when a young godchild struggles to understand the chaos in his world because of a sick grandparent. Maybe a godparent is there to cheer alongside mom or dad when the godson finishes elementary school. Or perhaps they begin regular e-mail or video chats with a teen goddaughter who is trying to make sense of injustice and violence she sees in her community. As families work through the ups and downs of life, godparents can provide invaluable, god-like support to their godchild, which can strengthen the entire family.

PREPARING GODPARENTS

Parents can honor the godparents they have chosen by naming the particular gifts those godparents have to bring to this child's life. Parents can further encourage godparents by welcoming them into their household and the life of their child, and including them in ordinary as well as extraordinary moments.

These are some ways godparents can prepare for the baptismal day and the life ahead:

❖ Before the baptism day, read through the entire baptismal service beginning on page 298, of the Book of Common Prayer, especially noting the vows you will take on behalf of your godchild.

❖ Take pictures as appropriate on the day of the baptism (most churches will not allow photography during the service—check with the priest). Consider saving pictures, bulletin, and other mementos in a scrapbook for your godchild.

❖ Find Bible storybooks or videos to share with your godchild.

❖ Sing songs or hymns. Children don't care if you can sing well; they just enjoy learning new songs and having fun!

❖ Go out of your way to acknowledge godchildren every time you see them. Children are sometimes unsure of how or when to approach, so take the initiative to greet them warmly and affectionately.

❖ As your godchild gets older, stay in touch *regularly*! It doesn't have to be long or elaborate but regular contact is important—phone call, text, e-mail, card, postcard, photo, trinket, smoke signal—the medium doesn't matter much; the regularity does. Also be sure your godchild knows how to reach you if they need you.

❖ Send cards or notes, not just on birthdays or holidays, but also (and especially) on the anniversary of their baptism date, reminding them again and again that they are a beloved child of God.

❖ Pray regularly for and with your godchild.

❖ Try to pay attention to the symbols of baptism so that as you encounter them you can mention them to your godchild and help teach them to watch for them too. Send an older child an e-mail from your beach trip to say, "I picked up a shell today and it reminded me of your baptism day," or call and say, "Today when it was raining, I watched the water splash and remembered the sound the water made as it was being poured into the font."

❖ Bake bread with your godchild or share a freshly baked piece. Talk about how bread is vital to most cultures and a powerful symbol of life.

❖ At some point in the later years of childhood or adolescence, it is possible your godchild may temporarily lose his or her way. Go see them face-to-face, if possible. Look them in the eyes. Hug them. Tell them you love them. Tell them God loves them. Remind them that they were "sealed by the Holy Spirit in baptism and marked as Christ's own forever." Even if they're not sure what they believe about those words at this particular point in life, promise them that you are still one hundred percent sure of how God feels about them. Remind them that whatever path they find themselves on, it is absolutely impossible for them to ever wander outside the realm of God's attention and affection.

About the Author:

Tracey E. Herzer is a Christian educator and formation specialist and, along with Nancy McLaughlin, the author of Godparenting: Nurturing the Next Generation. (Harrisburg, PA: Morehouse Publishing, 2007).

THE BAPTISMAL COVENANT

Now when they heard this, they were cut to the heart and said to Peter and to the other apostles, "Brothers, what should we do?" Peter said to them, "Repent, and be baptized every one of you in the name of Jesus Christ so that your sins may be forgiven; and you will receive the gift of the Holy Spirit. For the promise is for you, for your children, and for all who are far away, everyone whom the Lord our God calls to him." And he testified with many other arguments and exhorted them, saying, "Save yourselves from this corrupt generation." So those who welcomed his message were baptized, and that day about three thousand persons were added. They devoted themselves to the apostles' teaching and fellowship, to the breaking of bread and the prayers. —Acts 2:37–42

A central part of the baptismal rite, the Baptismal Covenant is both a statement of Christian belief and a guide to everyday living as a Christian. The Covenant consists of two main parts: first, three questions based on the Apostles' Creed, and second, five promises about living out the Christian faith. The church has a mission to bring the reconciling love of Christ to all the broken and hurting places of the world, and this mission is carried out by all of its members. The Baptismal Covenant helps Christians live into this mission in practical ways.

Ultimately, the Baptismal Covenant is about love. It encompasses our loving relationship with God, and directs us in how to show that love in the world. The baptized life is one of action, and the five promises of the covenant show us how to live out a life of faith. As we live into the Christian life all day, every day, we have opportunities to enact these promises in our households, congregations, neighborhoods, and the world.

The response to each of the five promises is, "I will with God's help." We are not left with the impossible burden of living a perfect life. Rather we are reminded that we always have God. We do not do these things on our own.

THE BAPTISMAL COVENANT

Celebrant Do you believe in God the Father?

People I believe in God, the Father almighty,
    creator of heaven and earth.

Celebrant Do you believe in Jesus Christ, the Son of God?

People I believe in Jesus Christ, his only Son, our Lord.
    He was conceived by the power of the Holy Spirit
      and born of the Virgin Mary.
    He suffered under Pontius Pilate,
      was crucified, died, and was buried.
    He descended to the dead.
    On the third day he rose again.
    He ascended into heaven,
      and is seated at the right hand of the Father.
    He will come again to judge the living and the dead.

Celebrant Do you believe in God the Holy Spirit?

People I believe in the Holy Spirit,
    the holy catholic Church,
    the communion of saints,
    the forgiveness of sins,
    the resurrection of the body,
    and the life everlasting.

Celebrant Will you continue in the apostles' teaching and fellowship, in the breaking of bread, and in the prayers?

People I will, with God's help.

Celebrant Will you persevere in resisting evil, and, whenever you fall into sin, repent and return to the Lord?

People I will, with God's help.

Celebrant Will you proclaim by word and example the Good News of God in Christ?

People I will, with God's help.

Celebrant Will you seek and serve Christ in all persons, loving your neighbor as yourself?

People I will, with God's help.

Celebrant Will you strive for justice and peace among all people, and respect the dignity of every human being?

People I will, with God's help.

LIVING THE BAPTISMAL COVENANT EVERY DAY

The Baptismal Covenant is to be lived out every day, in ordinary ways and ordinary places. Here are some practical suggestions:

❖ *Will you continue in the apostles' teaching and fellowship, in the breaking of the bread, and in the prayers?*

These practices were the direct response to baptism by those living in the time of the apostles, as expressed in the Acts of the Apostles (see above).

In the world: Actively participate in the life of a Christian congregation. Attend Bible studies, spiritual formation classes, and parish dinners. Be regular in worship; participation in the Eucharist is a renewal of baptism—the third part of the unified rite (bath-handlaying-communion). Practice prayer daily, for yourself, for others, for the world.

In the home: Read Bible stories. Learn together about the lives of the saints. Share family meals on a regular basis, and enjoy special feasts for Christian holy days. Say grace before meals and offer bedtime prayers.

❖ *Will you persevere in resisting evil, and,* whenever *you fall into sin, repent and return to the Lord?*

The words to note are "persevere" and "whenever." Baptism does not prevent anyone from sinning. Rather, it offers us the loving response: repent and return.

In the world: Learn to recognize temptations and actively resist hurtful and harmful behavior. Be willing to admit shortcomings, faults,

and sinfulness. Expect opportunities for reconciliation and act on them.

In the home: Teach children to accept responsibility for their actions and to apologize when they have hurt someone. Help them to understand what it means to say, "I am sorry," and to be sorry. Be willing to apologize and make amends to children when you have done the hurting. Be willing to apologize and make amends to the adults in your home when you have done the hurting.

❖ *Will you proclaim by word and example the Good News of God in Christ?*

The Christian life is good news. Great news. We share this news by what we do and what we say, how we say it, and to whom we say it. The good news is that Jesus loves us. The outrageous news is that we do not need to do anything to gain or earn this love; it is pure gift.

In the world: Do not be shy about being a Christian. Invite others to your parish for worship, a class, or a social event. Share your joy, love, and hope in the goodness of God's creation with others.

In the home: Tell children that Jesus loves them. Act like you know that Jesus loves you too.

❖ *Will you seek and serve Christ in all persons, loving your neighbor as yourself?*

Seek and serve. A baptized life is not about our close friends and us. It is about seeking out those who need love, and then offering our gifts to them. It is about expecting to find Christ in others: in people who we don't know, in people we don't like very much, in people who are quite different from us, in all people.

In the world: Notice people you would normally overlook and expect to find Christ in them. Look for opportunities to use your gifts to serve others. Be open to receiving the gifts of others. Volunteer in a soup kitchen, at your local school, or in a prison. Participate in a blood drive or a community improvement project. Expect to be changed by these activities.

In the home: Practice loving your neighbor down the street or across the world by loving the people you share a home with. Look for the image of Christ in those who live closest to you, in a bawling infant or a cranky teenager. Think of preparing a meal or assisting with homework as acts of loving service.

❖ *Will you strive for justice and peace among all people, and respect the dignity of every human being?*

No one is beyond the love of God. All people, regardless of their status or behavior, deserve to be treated with dignity.

In the world: Be aware of instances of injustice around you. Advocate for those with little power. Work against racism, poverty, and other social injustice. Recognize what privilege you hold and be willing to share it. Speak with courtesy and kindness to toll-booth workers, customer service folks, and children.

In the home: What would it look like to respect the dignity of every member of a household? Especially the youngest? Give all people in your household a voice and the opportunity to make important choices and contributions, regardless of age or ability. Teach children to negotiate and settle disputes with love and fairness.

The Baptismal Covenant is a lot to live in to and up to. It may be helpful to ponder the promises one at a time. Which seems most compelling? Which seems easy to live in to? Which seems to be the most challenging? Each time we renew our baptismal vows in the Baptismal Covenant, we encounter the opportunity to discover new ways to live more deeply into the Christian life.

THE EPISCOPAL BAPTISMAL RITE

Heavenly Father, we thank you that by water and the Holy Spirit you have bestowed upon these your servants the forgiveness of sin, and have raised them to the new life of grace. Sustain them, O Lord, in your Holy Spirit. Give them an inquiring and discerning heart, the courage to will and to persevere, a spirit to know and to love you, and the gift of joy and wonder in all your works. Amen. (BCP, p. 308)

In The Episcopal Church, baptism most appropriately takes place as part of a public celebration of the Eucharist on a Sunday morning or other feast day: the Easter Vigil; on the Day of Pentecost; on All Saints' Day, or the Sunday after All Saints' Day; or on the Feast of the Baptism of our Lord (the First Sunday after the Epiphany). Baptism is not a private affair; a person is baptized into the body of Christ, so it is important that the body is present. Also, the baptized life is not lived in isolation, but in relationship to Christian community. Community support is integral to the baptismal rite; all those present promise to uphold the newly baptized in their life in Christ.

The opening dialogue, or the first words of the service, reminds the gathered community of what baptism is all about, echoing words from the letter to the Ephesians 4:4–6:

> *There is one Body and One Spirit*
> *There is one hope in God's call to us*
> *One Lord, one Faith, one Baptism*

In The Episcopal Church, baptism is never repeated for an individual since it is understood as full initiation into the Christian life. Thus, those who have been baptized Christians in another denomination, using water and the triune formula, are welcomed as full members of the Body of Christ and are never re-baptized. Even those members who have left the church and return years later seeking renewal are offered the rite of Reaffirmation of Baptismal Vows rather than repeating the baptismal rite itself. The action God takes in baptism cannot be dissolved; thus the Episcopal rite of Baptism begins with the foundation of one Lord, one Faith, one Baptism.

After the opening dialogue, the service continues with the prayers, readings from scripture, and the sermon. This not only sets baptism in the context of regular eucharistic worship, but also reminds the community that any sacrament is imbedded in prayer and scripture.

PRESENTATION AND EXAMINATION OF THE CANDIDATES

Sponsors, faithful baptized Christians who have already begun to share this journey with them, first present the candidates. Those candidates who can speak for themselves are then asked, "Do you desire to be baptized?" while infants and young children have parents and godparents to speak for them. And so comes the moment to make the public commitment to this new life in Christ.

The examination follows, in the form of renunciations and acclamations. To be baptized is to enter into a new life, and these statements set the parameters for what that life is all about.

To renounce is to say "no" to, to turn away from. So the candidate is asked to renounce:

❖ Satan and all the spiritual forces that rebel against God;

❖ the evil powers of this world which corrupt and destroy the creatures of God;

❖ the sinful desires that draw us from the love of God.

But the baptized life is about much more than saying "no." It is also about saying "yes" to the love promised by Jesus and to turn toward that new life in Christ. So the candidate also promises:

❖ to turn to Jesus Christ and accept him as the savior;

❖ to put trust in Christ's grace and love;

❖ to follow and obey Jesus.

And then, the entire congregation, all who are gathered, the Body of Christ, pledges to support this person in her or his new life in Christ. The members of the congregation renew their own baptismal promises as they join the candidate in the Baptismal Covenant.

The Covenant is immediately followed by the Prayers for the Candidates, so that even before they are baptized, the candidates receive the prayerful support of the congregation.

THE BAPTISM

Finally, after all this preparation comes the baptism itself as the candidates and the celebrant move toward the font. The celebrant prays the Thanksgiving over the Water, blessing it. Each candidate is presented by name, and then the celebrant immerses, or pours water on, the candidate (depending on the tradition of that congregation) using the ancient words, "I baptize you in the name of the Father and of the Son and of the Holy Spirit."

Then, using chrism, oil that has be specifically blessed by the bishop for baptisms, the celebrant imposes hands and marks the sign of the cross on the forehead of the newly baptized, sealing the baptism and marking her as "Christ's own forever."

It is done. And there is more. Immediately the newly baptized are prayed over, the bishop or priest asking that God will, "Give them an inquiring and discerning heart, the courage to will and to persevere, a spirit to know and to love you, and the gift of joy and wonder in all your works." They are next publicly welcomed by the entire congregation, and immediately invited to share in communion and in the ongoing life of the baptized.

BAPTISM AND HOLY COMMUNION

Anyone who is baptized is welcome to receive communion, regardless of age. This is one of the results of understanding baptism as full initiation. Thus, there is nothing to prevent an infant receiving communion on the day of her baptism. Baptism is entrance into the Christian faith and life, and through communion that faith life is nurtured.

Sometimes parents and other adults believe that children should not receive communion until they can understand it. But, just like baptism, the Eucharist is a holy mystery. None of us, not even the greatest theologian, can adequately explain it. Rather, we are fed by it. We do not wait until children can understand the workings of the digestive system and the complexities of nutrition before we feed them. Sharing in Holy Communion, in the one bread and the one cup, is a significant way in which Christian faith is nurtured and the vehicle through which we enter deeply into communion with God. All of us are invited. All of us are made worthy through God's mercy. Each of us can experience the profound love of God through this sacrament and spend a lifetime reflecting on this experience.

REMEMBERING ONE'S BAPTISM

Q. What is the ministry of the laity?

A. The ministry of the lay persons is to represent Christ and his Church; to bear witness to him wherever they may be; and, according to the gifts given them, to carry on Christ's work of reconciliation in the world; and to take their place in the life, worship, and governance of the Church. (BCP, p. 855)

People are baptized at a particular time on a particular day in a particular place. But the baptized life is a continuous, developing relationship with Jesus Christ. Christians spend their entire lives living into their baptisms. To remember is to re-member, to call to mind or to be mindful again, to put something back together. Some people remember their baptismal day, and can call to mind the promises they made and the community of witnesses who surrounded them. They can draw on this experience, re-live it, and re-examine it as they continue to practice the Christian life. But even those who were baptized as infants can remember their baptisms. They too can be mindful of the promises made on their behalf, and can examine how they are living into their life in Christ.

The Episcopal Church teaches that all the baptized are ministers, and that laypeople have an important and particular part to play. With baptism comes responsibility. Laypeople, or the laity, are the non-ordained members of the church. The Episcopal Church recognizes four orders of ministry, and the laity is considered the primary order. Laypeople share with bishops, priests, and deacons the charge to "represent Christ and his Church." Being Christian is never a private affair.

Laypeople are also expected to bear witness to Christ "wherever they may be." This is the call to be an ordinary Christian—that is, to practice Christian teachings and values in all the ordinary times and places. Christians are to spread the love of Christ in the world and not just keep the good news to themselves. This means sharing that love on the subway and the highway, in the workplace and on the athletic field, in the grocery store and at the vacation resort.

The baptized are to "carry on Christ's work of reconciliation in the world." They are Christ's hands and feet in the here and now. This is why the Baptismal Covenant calls us to persevere in resisting evil, to seek Christ in all persons, to strive for justice and peace in the world. And it is assumed that laypeople have been given spiritual gifts to carry out this work. Spiritual gifts are named in scripture and they include attributes like wisdom, knowledge, faith, healing, teaching, and prayer (see 1 Corinthians 12, Romans 12, and Ephesians 4 for examples of spiritual gifts). Not everyone has the same gifts, but all of us have God-given capacities to minister in the world.

Part of remembering that one is baptized, of living into one's baptism, is to identify what particular gifts one has for serving others. . . and then use them. Some might use their gifts of teaching to lead a children's class at their parish or a literacy class at the local library. Others might use their expertise with finances to volunteer as the treasurer for a local charity. Whatever an individual's particular gifts are, when they are put to use to make the world a better place, then Christ's work is being carried out.

Remembering one's baptism also calls for us to continually strengthen our faith life through spiritual practices or disciplines. Such disciplines include prayer, fasting, the study of scripture, and giving. We also live into our baptisms by learning more about our faith. This can be done through reading scripture, being involved in Bible study or other classes, and intentional conversations with other Christians.

We strengthen our faith by participating in the Christian community. Christians are called to worship God together in community, and to share in the Eucharist. But Christian community is also found in church spaghetti suppers and youth car washes, which offer opportunities for fellowship and building relationships with others.

Other ways to remember one's baptism, whether a child or adult, might include:

❖ celebrating one's baptismal anniversary with prayers or a party;

❖ attending a spiritual retreat;

❖ keeping a journal;

❖ observing the seasons of the church year;

❖ participating in a church camp or vacation bible school.

However one chooses to live into the baptized life, it will always be living into the mystery.

BAPTISMAL INSTRUCTION

It shall be the duty of Rectors or Priests-in-Charge to ensure that persons be prepared for Baptism. Before baptizing infants or children, Rectors or Priests-in-Charge shall ensure the sponsors be prepared by instructing both the parents and the Godparents concerning the significance of Holy Baptism, the responsibilities of parents and Godparents for the Christian training of the baptized child, and how these obligations may properly be discharged.
(Canon III.9.5.b.3, Constitutions and Canons of The Episcopal Church 2012)

The sacrament of Holy Baptism is appropriately preceded by instruction and prayerful preparation. Providing such instruction is a canonical obligation for clergy in charge of congregations; it is essential to provide those about to enter into the holy mystery of baptism with information, loving guidance, and support. No one, regardless of age, can ever be fully instructed in the Christian faith before being baptized. Faith formation is a lifelong endeavor. The baptized spend their entire lives growing into the full stature of Christ. Nevertheless, one can be equipped to begin this journey, and having some instruction and the right tools always makes an expedition more successful.

Adults, parents, or young children may be asked to participate in any of the following activities as part of their baptismal preparation and instruction:

❖ Meet with the clergy as soon as possible to discuss the nature of baptism and any particular practices of the congregation. (You may be asked to fill out an application like the one included in this book.)

❖ Attend several classes for instruction. Hopefully your priest has been mindful of how to make these accessible for participants who may be adults with busy work schedules, or older children who have different learning needs, or the sleep deprived parents of infants.

❖ Learn about topics to include:
— the significance of Holy Baptism;
— the place of Holy Scripture;
— the importance of the creeds, corporate worship, and individual spiritual practices;
— the responsibilities of parents and godparents for raising a child in the faith;
— the role of lifelong formation in the faith;
— the components of the baptismal service.

❖ If there is more than one baptismal candidate, expect to attend classes with others, as people of all ages learn much from engaging with other seekers.

❖ Invite godparents to participate in the instruction.

❖ If you are an adult preparing for baptism, you may be requested to enroll in the catechumenate, using the "Preparation for Adults for Holy Baptism" found in the *Book of Occasional Services.*

❖ Receive other resources for further reading and preparation (such as what is listed on p. 49).

❖ Attend a rehearsal close to the day of the baptism.

THE IMPORTANCE OF REHEARSAL

Clergy and lay leaders are accustomed to the rhythm of liturgical rites, to speaking up in church, and to participating fully in community worship. This may not be true for baptismal candidates, sponsors, parents, or godparents. A well-run rehearsal is not only an additional opportunity for instruction in the faith, it is also an act of hospitality. Rehearsals are best done without haste and when possible should occur on a day other than the baptism itself.

Participants need to know where to sit, where and when to stand, and how to move smoothly into place. They need to know when, and how loudly, to speak up. They need to know how to follow the service using the service leaflet or the Book of Common Prayer. Walking through the service (rather than just talking through the service) with all the participants present is the best way to put people at ease so that on the day of the baptism itself the participants can be focused on the significance of the ritual rather than worrying about where and when to stand.

What if one parent is not Christian?

Since baptism of a child assumes that child will be raised in the Christian faith and life, parents who are raising a child together need to be in agreement about nurturing the spiritual life of their child. However, it is not necessary that both parents be Christian. Children can be immersed in the Christian faith and at the same time be taught to understand, respect, and appropriately participate in other faith traditions. A parent who is not Christian would not be one of the child's sponsors for baptism, as being a sponsor necessitates making a commitment to Christ; however, his or her presence would be very welcome.

What is the right thing to wear?

A baptism is a celebration of new life, so wearing something festive would be fitting. In the church, white is a traditional color representing new life. However there is no rule or rubric that dictates what color should be worn.

At what age should children be baptized?

Children can be baptized at any age. If parents intend to raise their children in the Christian faith, there is no reason to delay. The sooner a child is baptized, the sooner she can be formed by full inclusion in the faith community. As a practical consideration, parents of newly born or newly adopted infants might want to wait a few months so that all involved are able to participate in the ceremony joyfully.

How many godparents should (or can) a child have?

There is no set rule about the number of godparents a child should have. Two or three is a reasonable choice. Some congregations do provide guidelines about choosing godparents, so parents should check with their priest.

What if a godparent can't be present at the service?

Being present at the baptismal liturgy to sponsor a child is one of the most important roles of a godparent. Parents should make an effort to choose godparents who will be able to attend. But there are also significant godparenting tasks that take place throughout a child's life, and parents may wish to include a godparent who simply cannot be present at the baptism itself. Parents should check with their clergy about choosing godparents as many parishes have policies regarding this situation.

As an adult candidate, do I need a sponsor or godparent?

Adult candidates have sponsors rather than godparents. Sponsors are mature Christians who present the candidate during the baptismal rite and support the candidate in her or his life in Christ. Sponsors are typically members of the congregation to which the candidate belongs.

When are baptisms held?

According to the Book of Common Prayer, "Holy Baptism is appropriately administered within the Eucharist as the chief service on a Sunday or other feast" (p. 298). Private baptisms are not the practice in The Episcopal Church. Some parishes schedule baptisms on these especially appropriate feast days: the Easter Vigil, the Day of Pentecost, All Saints' Day (or the Sunday after All Saints' Day), and the Feast of the Baptism of Christ (which is the first Sunday after the Epiphany).

Can family and friends attend the baptism if they are not members of the church or Christians?

Family and friends who are not Christians or who are not members of the baptismal candidate's church are most welcome to attend the baptism and to participate in the liturgy as appropriate. The Episcopal Church welcomes all those who are baptized Christians, regardless of denomination, to receive communion.

SCRIPTURE READINGS

The lessons that will be read during the rite of Holy Baptism are typically the assigned readings of the Sunday according to the church's calendar. There will be a reading from the Hebrew Scriptures (Old Testament), followed by a psalm (either sung or read), a New Testament lesson, and a reading from one of the gospels. The following selections of scripture are also used at baptisms and may be useful for personal reflection.

FROM THE HEBREW SCRIPTURES

ISAIAH 55:1–11

Ho, everyone who thirsts,
    come to the waters;
and you that have no money,
    come, buy and eat!
Come, buy wine and milk
    without money and without price.
Why do you spend your money for that which
       is not bread,
    and your labor for that which does
      not satisfy?
Listen carefully to me, and eat what is good,
    and delight yourselves in rich food.
Incline your ear, and come to me;
    listen, so that you may live.
I will make with you an everlasting covenant,
    my steadfast, sure love for David.
See, I made him a witness to the peoples,
    a leader and commander for the peoples.
See, you shall call nations that you do not know,
    and nations that do not know you shall run
      to you,
because of the LORD your God, the
      Holy One of Israel,
    for he has glorified you.

Seek the LORD while he may be found,
    call upon him while he is near;
let the wicked forsake their way,
      and the unrighteous their thoughts;
let them return to the LORD, that he may have
    mercy on them,
    and to our God, for he will abundantly
      pardon.
For my thoughts are not your thoughts,
    nor are your ways my ways, says the LORD.
For as the heavens are higher than the earth,
    so are my ways higher than your ways
    and my thoughts than your thoughts.

For as the rain and the snow come down from
      heaven,
    and do not return there until they have
      watered the earth,
making it bring forth and sprout,
    giving seed to the sower and bread to the
      eater,
so shall my word be that goes out from my
      mouth;
    it shall not return to me empty,
but it shall accomplish that which I purpose,
    and succeed in the thing for which I sent it.

EZEKIEL 36:24–28

I will take you from the nations, and gather you from all the countries, and bring you into your own land.

I will sprinkle clean water upon you, and you shall be clean from all your uncleannesses, and from all your idols I will cleanse you. A new heart I will give you, and a new spirit I will put within you; and I will remove from your body the heart of stone and give you a heart of flesh. I will put my spirit within you, and make you follow my statutes and be careful to observe my ordinances. Then you shall live in the land that I gave to your ancestors; and you shall be my people, and I will be your God.

FROM THE PSALMS

PSALM 15

O Lord, who may dwell in your tabernacle? *
who may abide upon your holy hill?

Whoever leads a blameless life and does
what is right, *
who speaks the truth from his heart.

There is no guile upon his tongue;
he does no evil to his friend; *
he does not heap contempt upon
his neighbor.

In his sight the wicked is rejected, *
but he honors those who fear the Lord.

He has sworn to do no wrong *
and does not take back his word.

He does not give his money in hope of gain, *
Nor does he take a bribe against the
innocent.

Whoever does these things *
shall never be overthrown.

PSALM 23

The Lord is my shepherd; *
I shall not want.
He makes me lie down in green pastures *
and leads me beside still waters.

He revives my soul *
and guides me along right pathways for his
Name's sake.

Though I walk through the valley of the shadow
of death,
I shall fear no evil; *
for you are with me;
your rod and your staff, they comfort me.

You spread a table before me in the presence of
those who trouble me; *
you have anointed my head with oil,
and my cup is running over.

Surely your goodness and mercy shall follow me
all the days of my life, *
and I will dwell in the house of the
Lord for ever.

PSALM 42:1–9

As a deer longs for the water-brooks, *
so my soul longs for you, O God.

My soul is athirst for God, athirst for the
living God; *
when shall I come to appear before the
presence of God?

My tears have been my food day and night, *
while all day long they say to me,
"Where now is your God?"

I pour out my soul when I think on these things:*
how I went with the multitude and led them
into the house of God,

With the voice of praise and thanksgiving, *
Among those who keep holy–day.

Why are you so full of heaviness, O my soul? *
and why are you so disquieted within me?

Put your trust in God; *
>   for I will yet again give thanks to him,
>   who is the help of my countenance, and
>   my God.

My soul is heavy within me; *
>   therefore I will remember you from the land
>   of Jordan,
>   and from the peak of Mizar among the
>   heights of Hermon.

Our deep calls to another in the noise of your
>   cataracts; *
>   all your rapids and floods have gone over
>   me.

PSALM 84

How dear to me is your dwelling, O LORD of
>   hosts! *
>   My soul has a desire and longing for the
>   courts of the LORD;
>   my heart and my flesh rejoice in the living
>   God.

The sparrow has found her a house
and the swallow a nest where she may
>   lay her young; *
>   by the side of your altars, O LORD of hosts,
>   my King and my God.

Happy are they who dwell in your house! *
>   they will always be praising you.

Happy are the people whose strength is in you! *
>   whose hearts are set on the pilgrims' way.

Those who go through the desolate valley will
>   find it a place of springs; *
>   for the early rains have covered it with
>   pools of water.

They will climb from height to height; *
>   and the God of gods will reveal himself
>   in Zion.

LORD God of hosts, hear my prayer; *
>   harken, O God of Jacob.

Behold our defender, O God; *
>   and look upon the face of your Anointed.

For one day in your courts is better than
>   a thousand in my own room, *
>   and to stand at the threshold of the house
>   of my God
>   than to dwell in the tents of wicked.

For the LORD God is both sun and shield; *
>   he will give grace and glory;

No good thing will the LORD withhold; *
>   from those who walk with integrity.

O LORD of hosts, *
>   happy are they who put their trust
>   in you!

FROM THE NEW TESTAMENT

ROMANS 6:3–5

Do you not know that all of us who have been baptized into Christ Jesus were baptized into his death? Therefore we have been buried with him by baptism into death, so that, just as Christ was raised from the dead by the glory of the Father, so we too might walk in newness of life. For if we have been united with him in a death like his, we will certainly be united with him in a resurrection like his.

ROMANS 8:14–17

For all who are led by the Spirit of God are children of God. For you did not receive a spirit of slavery to fall back into fear, but you have received a spirit of adoption. When we cry, "Abba! Father!" it is that very Spirit bearing witness with our spirit that we are children of God, and if children, then heirs, heirs of God and joint heirs with Christ—if, in fact, we suffer with him so that we may also be glorified with him.

2 CORINTHIANS 5:17–20

So if anyone is in Christ, there is a new creation: everything old has passed away; see, everything has become new! All this is from God, who reconciled us to himself through Christ, and has given us the ministry of reconciliation; that is, in Christ God was reconciling the world to himself, not counting their trespasses against them, and entrusting the message of reconciliation to us. So we are ambassadors for Christ, since God is making his appeal through us; we entreat you on behalf of Christ, be reconciled to God.

FROM THE GOSPELS

MARK 1:9–11

In those days Jesus came from Nazareth of Galilee and was baptized by John in the Jordan. And just as he was coming up out of the water, he saw the heavens torn apart and the Spirit descending like a dove on him. And a voice came from heaven, "You are my Son, the Beloved; with you I am well pleased."

MARK 10:13–16

People were bringing little children to him in order that he might touch them; and the disciples spoke sternly to them. But when Jesus saw this, he was indignant and said to them, "Let the little children come to me; do not stop them; for it is to such as these that the kingdom of God belongs. Truly I tell you, whoever does not receive the kingdom of God as a little child will never enter it." And he took them up in his arms, laid his hands on them, and blessed them.

JOHN 3:1–6

Now there was a Pharisee named Nicodemus, a leader of the Jews. He came to Jesus by night and said to him, "Rabbi, we know that you are a teacher who has come from God; for no one can do these signs that you do apart from the presence of God." Jesus answered him, "Very truly, I tell you, no one can see the kingdom of God without being born from above." Nicodemus said to him, "How can anyone be born after having grown old? Can one enter a second time into the mother's womb and be born?" Jesus answered, "Very truly, I tell you, no one can enter the kingdom of God without being born of water and Spirit. What is born of the flesh is flesh, and what is born of the Spirit is spirit."

RESOURCES

FOR PARENTS AND CHILDREN

Barron, Helen. *Journey into Baptism* (Denver, CO: Candle Press, 2014). www.candlepress.com

Gittings, Valerie. *I Belong: My Baptism Scrapbook* (Harrisburg, PA: Morehouse Publishing, 2000).

Kitch, Anne E. *Taking the Plunge: Baptism and Parenting* (Harrisburg, PA: Morehouse Publishing, 2006).

_____. *Water of Baptism, Water for Life: An Activity Book* (New York: Morehouse Publishing, 2012).

McLaughlin, Nancy Ann and Tracey E. Herzer. *Godparenting: Nurturing the Next Generation* (Harrisburg, PA: Morehouse Publishing, 2007).

Pritchard, Gretchen Wolff. *New Life! The Sunday Paper's Baptism Book* (New Haven, CT: The Sunday Paper, 1986) www.the-sunday-paper.com

Wangerin, Walter and Gerardo Suzan. *Water, Come Down: The Day You Were Baptized* (Minneapolis, MN: Augsburg Books, 1999).

Westerhoff, John H., III. *Holy Baptism: A Guide for Parents and Godparents* (Harrisburg, PA: Morehouse Publishing, 1998).

FOR ADULTS

Finan, Jeanne. *Remember Your Baptism: Ten Meditations* (Boston: Cowley Publications, 2005).

Micks, Marianne H. *Deep Waters: An Introduction to Baptism* (Boston: Cowley Publications, 1996).

Stevenson, Kenneth E. *The Mystery of Baptism in the Anglican Tradition* (Harrisburg, PA: Morehouse Publishing, 1998).

Tammany, Klara. *Living Water: Baptism as a Way of Life* (New York: Church Publishing, 2002).

Westerhoff, Caroline A. *Calling: A Song for the Baptized* (New York: Seabury Books, 2004).

FOR INSTRUCTION

ChurchNext, online courses on baptism, www.churchnext.tv

"Concerning the Catechumenate" and "Preparation for Adults for Holy Baptism" found in the *Book of Occasional Services* (New York: Church Publishing, 1995).

Turrell, James F. *Celebrating the Rites of Initiation: A Practical Ceremonial Guide for Clergy and Other Liturgical Ministers* (New York: Church Publishing, 2013).

Wile, Mary Lee. *Christ's Own Forever: Episcopal Baptism of Infants and Young Children: Leader's Guide* and *Parent/Godparent Journal* (Denver, CO: Morehouse Education Resources, 2002, 2006).

GLOSSARY

All Saints' Day: November 1, a day when all the departed, especially those known to us, are remembered. Since the lives of the saints begin at baptism, this day, or the Sunday after it, is one of the appropriate times for baptism.

Baptism: The full initiation by water and the Holy Spirit into Christ's Body, the Church.

Baptismal Covenant: The rite of Christian initiation contains a series of vows, made by all present, called the "Baptismal Covenant" (BCP, p. 304–5).

Catechumen, Catechumenate: Candidates for baptism are called "catechumens," that is, persons under instruction. The catechumenate is the period of time during which candidates are prepared for baptism.

Chrism: Consecrated oil used for anointing the newly baptized person with the sign of the cross at baptism. At the consignation, the bishop or priest says to each newly baptized person, "You are sealed by the Holy Spirit in Baptism and marked as Christ's own forever" (BCP, p. 308). Olive oil mixed with fragrant oil, chrism is consecrated by a bishop for anointing purposes, such as baptism and at the time of death, by a priest.

Epiphany: January 6, the twelfth day of Christmas, is when the church celebrates the coming of the wise men, or magi, to the Christ Child. The theme of Epiphany season is the light of Christ shining out into the world. The first Sunday of the season celebrates Christ's baptism and is therefore an especially appropriate time for Christian baptism.

Eucharist: The sacrament of Christ's body and blood, and the principal act of Christian worship. The term is from the Greek word for "thanksgiving." In the Book of Common Prayer, the whole service is entitled the Holy Eucharist. The Eucharist is also called the Lord's Supper, Holy Communion, the Divine Liturgy, the Mass, and the Great Offering.

Font: The vessel in which baptism takes place, often on an eight-sided stand holding a basin, in which the water is poured during the rite of Holy Baptism. The eight sides symbolize what Christians have called the "eighth day" of creation, the day on which Christ rose from the dead beginning a re-creation of human life.

Grace: God's love freely given to humanity for salvation. By grace God "forgives our sins, enlightens our minds, stirs our hearts, and strengthens our wills" (BCP, p. 858).

Pascal Candle: The special candle lit at the Easter Vigil that burns throughout the Easter season as a symbol of the Light of Christ. The Pascal Candle is usually placed near the baptismal font and is lit at baptisms and funerals.

Pentecost: From the same root as "pentagon" ("five-sided"), the Feast of Pentecost is a Jewish festival celebrated fifty days after the Passover. It was on that day, approximately fifty days after Easter, that the apostles first received the gift of the Holy Spirit. The Feast of Pentecost and the long season following it call us to remember the gift of the Spirit and our need to follow the Holy Spirit's guidance. It is another appropriate time in the church year to celebrate baptisms.

Presbyter: The English word "priest" is derived from "presbyter," a minister who preaches the word and administers the sacraments.

Rite, Ritual: A form for religious ceremony that includes what is said and what is done in the religious observance. Rite expresses the church's relationship with God through words, actions, and symbols. It orders the church's common worship, enabling the community to share its faith and experience God's presence in a particular liturgical and pastoral context.

Sacrament: "An outward and visible sign of an inward and spiritual grace" (BCP, p. 857). Baptism and Eucharist are the principal sacraments in The Episcopal Church in which God acts in human lives. The outward sign of baptism is water, and the outward sign of the Eucharist is bread and wine.

Vigil: A service of watching, held on the evening before a major feast day. The Easter Vigil is the central service of the Christian year and an especially appropriate time for baptisms to take place.

CHECKLIST AND APPLICATION FORM

THINGS TO DO

❑ Schedule an appointment with a member of the clergy to discuss baptism.

Notes: _____

_____

❑ Notify the church office at the time of your child's birth or adoption (in the case of the baptism of an infant).

Notes: _____

_____

_____

❑ Discuss with your priest (or other appropriate person) your congregation's process for baptismal preparation, including classes, the selection of godparents or sponsors, and upcoming baptismal dates.

Notes: _____

_____

_____

❑ Review the baptismal process with clergy and before determining a date you desire for your (or your child's) baptism. (Some congregations have set dates.)

Notes: _____

_____

_____

❑ Complete and mail (or e-mail) your congregation's application form (or the form found in this booklet) to the church office.

Notes: _____

_____

❑ Attend the pre-baptismal classes.

Notes: _____

_____

_____

❑ Attend the baptismal rehearsal.

Notes: _____

_____

_____

APPLICATION FOR HOLY BAPTISM

Date of Application _____

Full Name of Candidate _____

Address of Candidate _____

_____

_____

Date of Birth_____

Place of Birth _____

If candidate is not an adult:

Parents' Full Names: Member of Church

1. _____   ☐ yes ☐ no

2. _____   ☐ yes ☐ no

Contact Information for Candidate or Parents:

Home: _____   Work: _____

Cell: _____   E-mail: _____

Statement of Commitment to be completed upon application by the Candidate or Parents:

I desire to be baptized/We desire that our child be baptized because

_____

_____

_____

_____

_____

_____

_____

_____

_____

_____

_____

_____

Signed   _____

_____

To be completed after discussion with clergy:

Requested Date of Baptism _____

Sponsors/Godparents:

1. _____

Church Affiliation _____

2. _____

Church Affiliation _____

3. _____

Church Affiliation _____

Mail, e-mail, or fax this completed application to the church administrator at:

For office use only:

Met with clergy (date) _____

Attended baptismal instruction (date) _____